Economics
Made Simple for the Young and Old

Professor Mike Clears Up The Myths

Michael Walcott

authorHOUSE®

AuthorHouse™
1663 Liberty Drive
Bloomington, IN 47403
www.authorhouse.com
Phone: 1-800-839-8640

First published by AuthorHouse 1/15/2010

ISBN: 978-1-4490-5023-8 (e)
ISBN: 978-1-4490-5022-1 (sc)

Library of Congress Control Number: 2009913743

Printed in the United States of America
Bloomington, Indiana

This book is printed on acid-free paper.

Dedication

This book is dedicated to my best friend, great economics teacher, and man of many interests, Dr Philip Gregorowicz who died on August 14, 2008 at the age of 62. Thanks Phil, for teaching me so much about economics and about the world.

INTRODUCTION

I first heard the word "**Economics**" when I was in high school in my native Guyana. I was about fourteen and my brother John was taking a course in economics. The word itself sounded **intimidating** to me, even though I didn't know what economics was. One day I picked up my brother's introductory economics textbook and started reading. To my surprise, it sounded like pure **common sense**. Since then I have taken numerous economics courses but I still haven't changed my mind about that little observation. I still think that it's nothing but **common sense!**

I have taught economics since 1983 when I joined the Department of Economics at Auburn University at Montgomery as an **instructor** of economics. Today, over twenty-six years later, I am still teaching **introductory** economics and having a great time making it simple for my students at Faulkner University in Montgomery, Alabama. After teaching economics for all these years, here is what I have discovered about the teaching and learning of economics:

1) Economics is **logical, commonsense,** and is based on **observing** the behavior of ordinary people like you and me.

2) Economics appears difficult because students approach it as if it is something very **mystical**, and some teachers do not help to **demystify** it.

3) Economics is one of the most important subjects that an American citizen (or world citizen, for that matter) ought to learn; yet it is not a required class in high school, or in most college degree plans.

4) Economics is the basis of our country's continued survival and its **political system**, but most educators and **policymakers** do not see it as important as Literature, English or History.

5) Because they do not understand the connection between **politics** and economics, people often vote for policies that are against their own **self-interest.**

Why did I write this book?

I wrote this book because I have complained since I started teaching over twenty-six years ago that Americans understand so little about the economic and business **environment** in which they were born and raised. They often have no clue and no interest in actions being taken on their behalf today; actions that will severely affect their future. As an example, the **national debt** (eleven trillion and rising) will almost certainly have to be repaid by the next three **generations** of Americans coming behind the **Baby Boomers,** (who won't be around for long enough to see that happy event!) Yet most twenty year olds don't know about it and don't care about it if they do know! After complaining for years and getting nowhere, I decided that I would myself write an economics book for young Americans.

I will try to keep American political **partisanship** out of the discussions unless it becomes necessary to explain concepts like "**voting your self interest**," or when explaining concepts directly related to the two **dominant** political parties in America. When I do give an **opinion,** I will make it clear that this is my opinion and not accepted economic law or theory.

I am neither a **Democrat** nor a **Republican**

and expect to stay so for the rest of my life. I find often that when people join political organizations, they give up the right to think for themselves. I have seen the damage that this **groupthink** has done to the American system of politics, and I refuse to be a part of that gridlock. I will try to keep things simple and **non-partisan**, I will try to keep it interesting for all readers but mostly for young readers. Happy reading!!

Note: *Items in bold will be defined and explained in the glossary at the end of the book.*

Contents

CHAPTER ONE –
What is Economics?

E conomics is the study of how ordinary people like you and me go about the business of living our lives in a world where there is not enough stuff to give everybody all that they want. People want food, houses, medicine, clothes, movies and all those other things that make life comfortable and interesting. But we don't find these things lying around on the ground for us to pick up. No! If we want them we'll have to make them. Well, studying economics helps us to figure out how to do this in the best and most **efficient** way for the benefit of lots of people. But how did all this economics stuff get started anyway? A look at a little history might be helpful.

In ancient times, long, long ago, people wandered around in small groups hunting for food and shelter wherever they could find it. Because they spent most of their time looking for food and shelter, there wasn't much time left for thinking. As time passed and people lived longer and grew smarter, they learned better ways to find food, make clothing from animal skins and furs and find shelter in caves. Over thousands of years, people got to be very good at providing for their needs, and after a while they decided to stay put in any place where food was **abundant** or where they could grow it themselves.

This development left people with extra time on their hands, so they started to think about ideas of how to make their methods more **efficient** and their lives more interesting. One of the important things they discovered is "**Demand and Supply!**" What this means is that everybody wants things to use, like food, clothes, houses and medicine. They are said to **demand** those things and are willing to pay somebody to make those things for them. A different group of people decided to produce things and sell them at a **profit** to those who want them. These days we call the people who demand goods **consumers**, and the ones who make the goods, we call **suppliers (or producers)**

An important part of economics is the understanding of the relationship between **demand, supply** and **price**. For instance, things that people want very much (high demand) tend to have high prices, while things that they don't want much of (low demand) tend to have low prices. Something similar applies to supply. Things that are available in great quantities (high supply) tend to have low prices while things that are available only in small quantities (low supply) tend to have high prices.

Think of water, of which we (in the **West**) have

an **abundant** supply; the price is low! Now think of diamonds, of which we have a very small supply; the price is high! The forces of demand and supply together set the prices of things. Prices usually go up or go down when either demand or supply of anything changes. The **economy** of a country is the means by which the country chooses to meet the needs and wants of its people. Not all countries agree on the best approach to meet those needs and wants.

Some countries choose to let the government take the biggest role in organizing their economy. Such countries are called **socialist** countries, like Cuba and North Korea. They have little use for the **market** in setting **priorities** about what to produce and how to set a price on it.

On the other hand, some countries chose to let the government take a much smaller role in organizing the economy. Those countries are called **capitalist** countries. They depend on the **market** to decide what to produce and how to produce it. Why did different countries make different choices about their economies? Well, their peculiar histories led them to prefer one type of economy and distrust the other.

America has had a long history of using markets to make economic **decisions** and as a result has become one of the richest countries in the world. The socialist countries have not done as well in terms of providing for their people's need for food, housing, clothing, medicine etc. and are not as **materially wealthy** as the capitalist countries like America, Japan or Germany. As a result, many of those socialist countries have been trying to change their **methods of production** and **marketing**, becoming more like capitalists.

But even in the capitalist countries like ours, the market has been unable or unwilling to provide some types of services that most people agree we need. The government therefore has to provide such services or they may not be provided at all; examples are: **defense of the country against foreign invasion, social security and medical care for the elderly, education and public health for the people, courts, fire and police protection**.

But how does a country pay for these things? In order to pay for these services, the government has to ask people to pay taxes. There are three main types of taxes; **income taxes, property taxes** and **sales taxes**. The **federal government** gets most of its revenue from **income taxes** while **state and local governments** depend more heavily on **sales taxes** and **property taxes.**

Why are some people unwilling to pay **taxes** for services that most Americans agree the country needs? Well, some people believe the market can provide many of these services more efficiently than the government. Other people believe that if the government didn't provide these **services** they wouldn't be provided. That is a big part of the disagreement between the people who call themselves **conservatives** and those who call themselves **liberals**.

If you are a person who would like to see those services provided by the market you may be called a conservative! If you want the government to provide such services, you may be called a liberal. It is a difference of **opinion**, not a badge of **honor** or **dishonor!**

Why do some people want government help and others not want it? It seems to be mostly a matter of **income** and **wealth**. Those with low incomes, (usually called **poor** people) tend to look to the government for help. Those with high incomes, (usually called **rich** people), don't need or want government help. They feel they can provide for themselves and their families without any help from the government.

Those with low incomes have less ability to provide for themselves and may seek help from the government.

(**Opinion**) *I have yet to find unemployed or homeless persons who will refuse government assistance for food or shelter. You also will have a hard time finding rich people (who pay a lot of taxes) who are happy to see their taxes used to help people whom they often see as lazy or unmotivated.*

At different times in history, one or the other of these philosophies becomes more or less popular in America. In recent years most Americans have been identifying themselves as Conservatives, while few wanted to be called liberals. The word **liberal** has actually been treated like a dirty word since about the nineteen eighties.

At the time of this writing, (Spring 2009), the economies of America and the world are going through massive **convulsions** and people are scared and uncertain about their futures. In America, **unemployment** is rising rapidly as consumers and business firms have drastically cut their spending. Conservatives don't want to see the government borrow and spend **trillions** of dollars to fix the economy. Liberals want the government to borrow and spend money to get the economy going again so their jobs can come back. People normally want to buy houses, cars, education, clothes and vacations, but not when they know they might lose their jobs in the next few months!

The changing attitude about liberal and conservative beliefs is closely related to the problems of the recession and job losses. As unemployment gets higher, and more people find themselves in poverty, attitudes become more liberal and less conservative. The rich will hold on to their conservative beliefs because they will be fine regardless of what happens to the economy. They are always able to take care of their own needs. Rich people, if they were to become poor, are quite likely to change many of their views and attitudes.

This explains the major difference between the so-called **right (conservatives)** and **left (liberals)** of American politics. I will return to this topic later. For now, **Chapter Two** will let us look at how people make personal **choices** and how these choices affect their lives.

CHAPTER TWO –
Consumers and why we choose the things we do

Everybody wants to live a happy life full of good things like food, clothes, a nice home, televisions, computers etc. for us and our families. To satisfy these needs and wants, somebody has to **produce** goods and services. Those **producers** sell their goods to others called **consumers** at a price that will make for them a **profit.** To pay for the goods, most consumers get **money** by working at jobs for **wages.** They use their wages to buy the things that they think will make them happy. Both the buyer and seller have to agree on the price, then a sale can take place. After the sale, both parties are better off than they were before, or else why would they ever want to do it?

People want to be happy, so they try to find happiness in any way they can. Some people find it in religious pursuits, others in educational pursuits, others in sports etc. Some people find happiness in creating and **accumulating** large amounts of money. Most people buy things that they think will make them happy. This love of buying is a happy convenience for the American economy, because it keeps the economy working. Fortunately, the American people are usually happy to oblige.

Happiness, however, can be a confusing thing. It seems that for some people, no matter how much stuff they accumulate they never seem to get enough to make them happy. This creates a situation where people do not find what they are looking for in the stuff they buy. Let me expand on this business of satisfaction! It will help if I explain how **satisfaction** is gained when we consume goods.

When we use the first unit of a good, it gives us the greatest amount of satisfaction. The second unit gives us less satisfaction than the first, and the third gives us less satisfaction than the second and so on. (*Check it out and see if you feel the same way*). Because each successive unit gives us less satisfaction, when we have things in **abundance**, we place little value on the last unit we consume.

This phenomenon is called **The Law of Diminishing Marginal Utility** and explains why when you go into a candy factory and you are surrounded by the sight and smell of candy, you lose interest in candy. It also explains why when Americans peel a potato they leave an eighth of an inch thick layer of flesh still attached to the skin while people in Africa actually eat the whole potato including the skin. Why? There is great

abundance of potatoes in America, and great **scarcity** of potatoes in Africa.

Another example of this behavior is how we put a huge glob of toothpaste on our toothbrush when the tube of toothpaste is new, but skimp on the toothpaste when the tube is almost empty. Abundance versus **scarcity** is the explanation!

Another concept that explains human buying behavior is called **Elasticity of Demand. Elasticity of demand** for a product helps explain why consumers react in **predictable** ways when prices of some goods change. When the price of gasoline increases, people hardly change how much they buy. That is because gasoline is a **necessity** and has no known substitutes. On the other hand, when the price of apple juice rises, many people will quit buying apple juice and switch to orange juice or some other type of drink. That is because apple juice is not a necessity, and there are many other goods that can take its place.

Because of this phenomenon, when state governments need money, they will often place a heavy tax on gasoline, a necessity! They would not get much **revenue** from taxing Kool aid! People will pay any price for gasoline, but not for a sweetened drink.

An important question that many economics texts fail to ask is this! **"Why do American citizens become such avid consumers, but fail to recognize that not spending (saving) is also a**

source of great personal satisfaction?" The answer is that we, as children, start out early watching Saturday morning cartoons, **commercials** and other programs chock full with **advertising**. We are encouraged to spend and buy from birth onward. We learn early to try to get lots of stuff that we hope will make us happy.

However, few people, not even parents, spend any time teaching us that there is also satisfaction to be gained from not spending, but saving. There is a lot of evidence to demonstrate the virtues of saving. Most people are not aware of it, however. *Saving today gives us the chance to enjoy more spending tomorrow.*

Let me give you an example using numbers that you can check for yourselves with a business calculator. Suppose your grandfather died and left you $20,000 in his will when you are age eighteen. You can do two things with the money: spend it all now and get **immediate** satisfaction, or save it all and get much greater satisfaction at a future date.

There is a third option, which an eighteen year old will find more **palatable**; spend $10,000 for some immediate enjoyment, then invest the rest in a **mutual fund** or some other safe **investment instrument**. If the account receives an **annual return** of 8%, after 47 years, (by which time you are 65 years old) the $10,000 would have grown to become $372,000! You can retire comfortably on that. (Using a 10% rate of return would have made it $882,000)

Does this seem astounding? Well, that is because of a process called **compound interest**, which seems magical when applied to long periods of time. Ever heard of **Peter Minuit**? He was the Dutch governor of New York who around 1627 purchased Manhattan Island from the Indians for $24 worth of **trinkets**! Quite a bargain for Peter Minuit!! Well, imagine if the Indians could have invested that $24 in an account that paid 10% for 382 years (2009 minus 1627) they would have in their account today $156,000,000,000,000,000! (That is $156,000 **trillion,** more than what all of the **United States** is worth today!)

CHAPTER THREE –
Business fluctuations and how the government deals with them

We learned in Chapter One about people's need for goods that can make their lives enjoyable. Some method had to be created to produce those goods efficiently. To gain an understanding about how production works, we need to know about the factors of production.

There are four factors (or **resources**) that are necessary to produce things in an economy; **Land, Labor, Capital** and **Entrepreneurship**. You are most likely familiar with land and labor. Most people work for a living by **leasing** out their labor to those business people who need it. They will earn **wages** from **working** at a job. Other people own **land,** which they lease out to **business firms,** which will pay them **rent.**

The factors that you are probably less familiar with are **capital** and **entrepreneurship**. Those people who go into business for themselves are said to be leasing their entrepreneurship (**management skills**) and they earn **profit** when they are successful (**loss** when they are not successful). When a person saves his money in a bank, the bank uses this money to lend to others as **Capital,** and the owner of the money is paid **interest.**

This is all demonstrated in the model below, called the **circular flow of income**. It shows households leasing the four factors of production (**land, labor, capital and entrepreneurship**) to the business firms which pay them **rent, wages, interest and profit**. Households use the money received to buy from business firms the things they need, i.e. goods and services.

The Circular Flow of Income

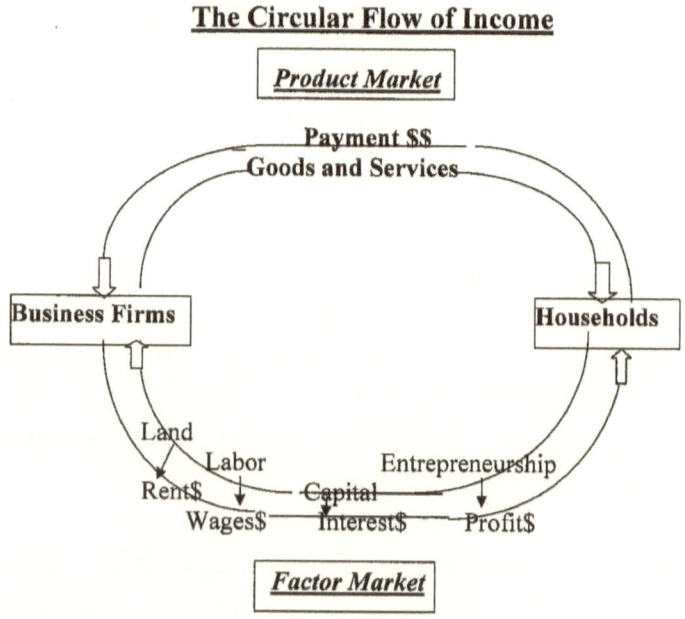

This simple model shows the outer wheel (called

the **financial wheel**) turning at the same rate as the inner wheel (the **real wheel**). Left alone, these two wheels will turn at a rate that suits conditions in the market.

What happens then, when market conditions cause the wheel to turn too slowly for the people's liking? Well, in that situation, (called a **recession**) the government steps in to speed things up by **stimulating** spending. Occasionally the wheels will turn too rapidly. This causes **inflation, (rising prices**)! Again, the government steps in to slow down the wheels in order to control the inflation.

If we lived in a perfect world, the economy would never slow down and cause recession, nor speed up and cause inflation. But, alas, the world is imperfect and we have to find **non-market** ways to get the economic wheels turning at a rate that is desirable.

This brings us to the subject of, "**What do we mean by desirable?**"

As you might expect, not everyone agrees on this, but most people desire to have low inflation and low unemployment. Can you see why this is desirable? Well think of your parents, who might both be working to feed, clothe and educate you. Suppose they were to lose their jobs (high **unemployment**)? They would be unable to provide for themselves and their children and this would make them unhappy!

On the other hand, suppose that prices of food,

clothes, gasoline, utilities, all started to rise rapidly (high **inflation**). Again, your parents would be unhappy because their limited income cannot buy as much as it used to buy before, causing their living standards to fall. Nobody wants that!! So the people in charge of the economy, the **Government**, try to find ways of keeping the wheels turning at the best rate to produce low unemployment and low inflation!

In theory, the government wants to please the largest number of people in the country. It is impossible however, to please everybody. This is where the political disagreements usually get started. Politics and economics are closely related because our candidates usually appeal for our votes using primarily **economic arguments**. They appeal to our **self-interest** to get us to vote for them. **Well-informed voters** try to find out what the candidates stand for, and vote for candidates who they think can govern in their (the voter's) self-interest. Now let us see what people usually ask of their candidates for office.

In order to better understand the next topic, (**government actions to regulate the economy**), we need to have a grasp of **unemployment** and its consequences. Americans receive the majority of their income from wages, earned from jobs offered by business firms. If for some reason those business firms cannot sell their products, they are forced to cut production and lay off workers. This creates higher unemployment!

When the economic wheels are turning well and all sectors are buying lots of stuff, the unemployment rate can get very low, but never zero! Even in the best of times it never reaches zero! Why? Because there are actually three types of unemployment and only one responds to government actions. They are: **Frictional Unemployment, Structural Unemployment**, and **Cyclical Unemployment.**

Frictional Unemployment is caused by people being temporarily between jobs. Because it takes time to move from one job to another, it will take even highly skilled workers four to twenty weeks to find another job. All this time they are unemployed and they are counted as such. **Structural unemployment** is caused by people having no needed skills, skills located in the **wrong place**, or skills that have become **obsolete**. These two types of unemployment will always be with us because there will always be people who quit jobs or are fired, and there will always be skilled people who live in places where the jobs no longer exist. That represents about a **3.5% to 4%** unemployment rate.

The unemployment that we have to worry about the most is **Cyclical Unemployment**. The name comes from the term **Business Cycle**. This type of unemployment is caused by a slowdown or recession in the economy. Why can't we stop the slowdown in the economy? In the previous paragraphs we said that households buy the goods and services that keep the economy going. Well, that was an over **simplification**. Actually, the economy depends on spending by **households, business firms**, the **federal government** and the **foreign sector** to keep it going.

To measure the economy's production, economists use a measure called the **Gross Domestic Product (GDP),** the total value of all final goods produced in a year. It is constructed by adding together household purchases (**Consumption**) plus business firm purchases (**Investment**) plus federal government purchases (**Government Spending**) plus foreign sector purchases (**Exports minus Imports**). In abbreviated form it looks like this:

C + I + G +(X-Im) = GDP.

To keep the economic wheels turning at the desired speed, all those components need to keep spending. If they stop spending for any reason, the economy goes into a recession. When that happens it is usually characterized by a decrease in **consumption**, followed by a decrease in business **investment**. After all, why would business firms want to invest in new production facilities if they can't sell the goods they are already producing?

Now consider the foreign sector, **imports** and **exports**. In a recession, Americans buy fewer imported goods while foreigners buy fewer of our goods. This means that during a recession, almost every component of **GDP** is decreasing. What's left? **Government Spending!**

Suppose the government were to do nothing about this situation! **GDP** would logically continue further downward, making the recession worse and worse. Neither households (which are losing jobs) nor business firms (which are not selling much product) can be depended on to drive spending back up. And we can't depend on sales to other countries because they are having similar problems to us. What can be done to turn this situation around??

Well, the government is the only player left in this game who has any power!! **Fiscal Policy** and **Monetary Policy** are the main means at the government's disposal to fight a recession. Fiscal policy uses **taxes** and government spending to stimulate the economy. The government can cut **personal taxes** to stimulate household spending. As households pay fewer taxes, they have more **disposable** income, so they spend it, increasing Consumption. The government can cut **business taxes**, increasing the business firms' disposable income. Business firms will then invest money in new plant and equipment i.e. increased investment.

Monetary policy uses interest rates and money supply to stimulate the economy. The **Federal Reserve Bank** is in control of this. The **Fed** (that's its nickname) will increase the **supply of money** and lower **interest rates**. This makes it cheaper for households and business firms to borrow money for homes, cars, education, new buildings, machinery, and to hire and train new workers. This increased spending by households and business firms will stimulate the economy to grow.

However, for the greatest and most direct effect on the economy, the federal government (using fiscal policy) will also add increased government spending. This adds to the stimulating effects of the other spending and causes the economy to **grow more rapidly**. But wait! There is a **catch**!

When you cut household taxes and business taxes, will tax **revenue** go down? **Of course, it will**! If at the same time that tax revenue decreases, government spending increases, what do you think will happen? You probably guessed it! The government will overspend (called a **budget deficit**) and will then have to borrow money to pay its bills. This adds to the **National Debt (Government Debt).**

Is this debt a burden on the federal government? Well, it could be, depending on how large it becomes and what kind of strain it puts on the economy. You could think of a similar situation; your house payment and the debt you owe on the house! Is this debt a burden for you? It depends on how big a strain on your income the payments are, and whether you need a house that size!

Debt on a house big enough to house your

family, with a payment that takes not too much from your income is considered **manageable debt (no more than 28% of your income)**. You have to live somewhere and you **are** making the payments comfortably. However, if the house is twice as big as you need and the payment twice as large as you can afford, then this is a problem. Can America **afford** its debt? Is its house too large? To answer that, we will need more information, which we will be providing in a later chapter. Let it suffice to say for now, that America took 204 years (1776 to 1980) to accumulate its first trillion dollars of debt. The next eleven trillion dollars took 29 years (from 1980 to 2009)! Is that a comforting thought?

CHAPTER FOUR -
The Great Depression and its similarities to 2009

The **Great Depression** was a period of time when the economies of America and the world slowed to a crawl that lasted for twelve years, 1929 through 1941, with small interruptions. What originally caused the Great Depression is not fully understood, but what happened during that time is well documented. Starting in August of 1929 consumer spending decreased rapidly and investment spending soon followed. When the **stock market crashed** in October it confirmed what people had been thinking, that the economy was slipping into a recession, and things got worse.

Without going into excessive detail, what happened was that after GDP started to fall, Americans lost faith in their banks and started to withdraw their money in a **panic!** Naturally, the banks did not have all the depositors' money at hand and many went **bankrupt**. The bank **failures** made it impossible for many businesses to pay their workers wages, business expenses etc. and businesses failed in huge numbers. Like a snowball rolling down a hill the depression got worse and worse. During the great Depression, unemployment reached 25%, while GDP fell nearly 60%.

In the 1930's, a British economist named **Keynes** recommended that the American government undertake massive spending programs to **stimulate** the economy. The government did increase spending a bit, but it was not enough to completely solve the problem. The economy recovered somewhat in 1936, but fell back again when the **stimulus** spending was cut back in 1937.

No one knows how long it would have taken to grow the economy out of the depression, but America entered the **Second World War** in December 1941. Japan attacked **Pearl Harbor**, and America declared war on both Japan and Germany. Within months the Great Depression was over as the American government spent massive amounts of money to fight the war in Asia and Europe. Think of what it must have taken to **outfit** an army of ten million men and women, with clothing, food, housing, guns, ammunition, tanks, ships, airplanes, cars and trucks. To supply all these things required the entire American **workforce** to get to work immediately. Within months the depression was over and the unemployment rate fell to 1.8%, the lowest it has ever been.

One of the unforeseen effects of the war was

that women entered the labor force by the millions and they have never left. In the thirties, before America entered the war, it was common for women to stay at home and take care of their husbands and children. The war created a new industry, **daycare**, so that mothers could have some place to leave their children during the day when both the parents were working.

How does the Depression experience compare with what's happening today? Well, so far in 2009, GDP has declined only about 6%, not 60%, and the banks have been rescued by **FDIC**, the **Federal Reserve** and the **Treasury Department**. In the worst part of the Depression unemployment rose to nearly 25%, today it is only 8.5%. Though the number of housing **foreclosures** is quite high today and the number of business failures is great, it is nowhere near as high as during the Great Depression. However, our recession is only about a year old, not twelve years, and we are not sure when the economy will hit bottom and turn around. In other words, it may get worse yet!

The current **Chairman of the Federal Reserve, Ben Bernanke** has stated that the reason the great depression was so severe was that so many banks were allowed to fail. In today's recession, the Fed has made massive efforts to rescue the banks, even though it was unpopular with voters to do so. But without the banks making loans to business and households, housing sales and new business ventures would grind to a halt, and a feeling of pessimism would overtake the nation!

This is the major problem that the government has to fight in 2009, this feeling of **pessimism**! When will it end? Only time will tell how long this lack of confidence in the banks, investments and markets in general will continue. One area of disagreement between the right and the left is the use of government spending. The **Left** wants it, lots of it, while the **Right** believes that the economy can solve itself without any help from the government. Who is right? Well, let us use a law of physics to try to explain what is likely to happen if there was no government intervention.

The components of GDP in 2008 were: Consumption, (70%), Government Spending, (20%), Investment, (14%), and Net Exports (-4%). When Consumption starts to decline, Investment immediately follows, because business inventories start piling up and businesses will no longer have an incentive to invest. The result is an accelerating downward movement of GDP, a deepening recession and increasing unemployment.

Newton's First Law of Motion in Physics states that a moving object will continue to move in the same direction unless an outside force is applied in the opposite direction. The same way, when Consumption and Investment start moving down, they will continue to decline unless some large enough force acts against the downward movement. **That force is Government Spending!** How do we know that?

We know this because there is no other force available that is powerful enough to turn around this massive economy. Without significant government spending, the recession deepens until it becomes Depression!

The discussions in this chapter dealt with **Fiscal Policy,** which deals with taxes and government spending. There is another important component of the arsenal of tools available to the country to fight recessions. It is called **Monetary Policy.** We shall discuss that topic and also how money is created in the next chapter.

CHAPTER FIVE -
Money, how it is created and are there limits to its creation

Let us begin with a simple question. Is money wealth? Well, as simple as it seems, there are two correct answers to that question. The first and more obvious answer is **"Yes!"** In a stable economy with normal economic conditions, a person who has a lot of money is certainly wealthy. However, if we agree that money is wealth, why then can't the government print up enough money to make every citizen a rich millionaire and let everyone go to the beach and live like a king, with servants and big houses?

It is quite clear that this would not work! With the same amount of goods and services available to be purchased but a huge increase in printed money, **prices** will increase, not **wealth**. Inflation would be the result. This is because true wealth is goods and services. Money is a **convenience** for making trades.

Before money was invented, people traded through **barter** (the exchange of goods for goods).

But barter was inconvenient! It requires a **double coincidence of wants**. This means that each person has to want what the other has. For instance, if Mary has shoes and wants meat, while Joan has meat, but wants blouses, they cannot trade. However, if Mary has shoes and wants meat, and Joan has meat and wants shoes, they can trade. This requirement makes it inconvenient because each person has to seek out two conditions to fulfill the trade.

Now imagine if all traders sold their goods for money! They can then use the money to buy whatever they want. No more double coincidence of wants! This is much more convenient. This particular function of money is called **a medium of exchange.** A medium of exchange means that each trader sells his goods for money and buys whatever he wants from other traders with the money.

There are two other important functions of money: a **unit of account**, and a **store of value.** A unit of account means that each good is priced in terms of the money rather than in terms of other goods. Because we have grown up seeing money used everyday, we are unaware of what the world would be like if there was no money.

Imagine a country with only four goods to trade: **shoes, shirts, suits and bicycles**. Suppose the exchange value of a pair of shoes is 6 shirts! Then the exchange value of a shirt is 1/6 pair of shoes. Suppose a suit has an exchange value of 8 pairs of shoes. A suit will have an exchange value of 48 shirts and a shirt will have an exchange value of 1/48 suit. A pair of shoes will have an exchange value of 1/8 suit. Do I have to continue with bicycles to demonstrate just how confusing this can become? With all items priced in dollars we know a shirt is valued at x dollars, a pair of shoes is 6x dollars and a suit is 48x dollars. This is much, much more convenient.

The third function of money is as a **store of value**. This means that with a money system you can sell your produce for money and save the money for future use rather than saving up the actual **commodity** to use years from now.

Throughout history mankind has found many strange objects to use as money, including rocks, beads, salt, milk, cattle, slaves and of course gold and silver. In modern times we use paper money, checks and electronic methods to conduct trade. To get from gold and beads to paper money and checks requires a little history lesson. In Europe during the **middle Ages, Goldsmiths** were pillars of the community and were trusted to hold people's valuables for safe keeping. They also possessed vaults that were difficult for thieves to break into. People used to leave their valuables, including gold, with the goldsmiths, paying a fee for service. After many years it dawned on the goldsmiths that some people would leave their valuables in the vault for many, many years before they would ever return to pick them up. The goldsmiths fell on the idea of lending out portions of these valuables while holding a portion in reserve.

Because of fear of robbers, the people who borrowed from the goldsmith didn't want to take their loans in actual gold, which jingled in their pockets! Instead, they took hand written receipts that promised to pay to the bearer of the note a specific amount of gold. The notes were signed by the goldsmith. Merchants would accept these receipts in place of gold, so these receipts became the world's first checks. Another development created the circumstance where the goldsmiths actually started to create more money than the gold they kept in their vaults.

Because borrowers took handwritten receipts and didn't take the actual gold, the goldsmith would return the gold to the vault and treat it like a new deposit of gold. He would then hold a part in reserve and lend out the rest, over and over again. Because borrowers used the borrowed gold receipts to make purchases, the goldsmiths were actually creating spending power. See the example below.

Gold Deposits	Reserve (10%)	Loans (90%)
1000 ozs	100 ozs	900 ozs
900 ozs	90 ozs	810 ozs
810 ozs	81 ozs	729 ozs

This process can continue until the 1000 ozs of gold can become 10,000 ozs of spending power.

Banks use the same approach today to create money. Imagine a bank that is started with total deposits of $1,000,000. See example below.

Deposits	Required Reserve (10%)	Loans (90%)
$1,000,000	$100,000	$900,000
$900,000	$90,000	$810,000
$810,000	$81,000	$729,000

The original deposit has the potential to grow to $10,000,000 in spending power. (1/.10 * $1,000,000 = $10,000,000). The Federal Reserve Bank sets the minimum reserve required by law. The actual minimum reserve these days is more like 3%.

In the early days of banking, governments used to keep actual reserves of gold in Treasury vaults to back their currency. Today, however, the American currency is backed by nothing but the faith of the users rather than any actual asset, gold or otherwise. Faith is the key to any stable currency. Imagine if the users of US dollars were to suddenly start to believe that merchants, banks and other businesses are not accepting dollars. Nobody would want to accept dollars as payment!

How do we control the money supply so that it does not lose its buying power? By keeping the supply of money in line with the production of goods and services, which, remember is what money promises to deliver.

When large amounts of money are created

without a commensurate increase in the quantity of goods and services produced, inflation sets in and the money loses its buying power. Zimbabwe in East Africa is learning this lesson today. Its inflation rate is running at two million percent, mainly because the government is creating huge amounts of Zimbabwean dollars, while there is no commensurate increase in the production of goods. Because production is so low, and dollars are so many, inflation eats away at the value of the Zimbabwean dollar. Does America face such a risk? **Hardly, unless we got crazy and deregulated the banks!**

The United States federal government for sixty years has been spending way above its tax revenues, creating a **federal budget deficit** almost every year. However, the government usually makes up its shortfall by borrowing money mostly from foreign countries like China, Japan and Saudi Arabia. This unceasing borrowing has resulted in a **Government Debt** of over **eleven trillion dollars.** But why would these countries continue to lend us so much money?

It is because these countries have such great **faith** in the US economy and in its **currency.** They continue to buy our government **securities**, mainly because they feel that their investment is safe in America and they are getting a good return on their investments. America has to be careful, however, because all it takes to wreck this arrangement is for lenders around the world to start believing that the US might become unable to pay its debts. Then faith in the dollar could be lost and America would no longer be able to finance its deficit spending with borrowed money. Then we'll be in real trouble!

CHAPTER SIX -
Labor, labor unions
and their history

The majority of Americans earn their income from wages earned on jobs. In early American history, there were many **immigrant**s from all over the world entering America looking for work. Wages were low and working conditions were very poor. The average worker worked about sixty hours per week in dirty, unsafe working conditions at the mercy of the extremes of temperature. Any worker who tried to demand better working conditions would be threatened with dismissal and replacement with one of the millions of immigrants always seeking work in America's factories.

In America and Europe, workers demanded better working conditions and formed **trade unions** to better bargain for them. The employers were not happy about the unions and used every means of blocking them, sometimes even resorting to violence against workers. In the early 1900's, the Congress passed legislation giving workers the right to organize into unions and to **strike** for better pay and **benefits.** Congress also passed laws limiting the workweek to forty hours.

As America became more industrialized, productivity rose and business firms became more profitable. Through laws and union bargaining, American workers became the highest paid in the world. Over the past hundred years the American middle class grew as workers began investing in stocks and bonds of some of the companies they worked for. In other words, workers' interests and the companies' interests began to converge.

Recently, in some parts of America, unions lost influence and membership, especially in the South. In recent years many people actually started to believe that there is no longer any need for unions, and some states passed laws discouraging union organizing. Only time will tell just how accurate the notion is that workers will do fine without unions to represent them.

Union agitation as well as laws passed during and after the great depression helped to reduce the gap between the rich and the poor. The suffering that Americans went through during the Great Depression also caused Congress to pass several pieces of legislation that today would be called liberal and might not even get a chance to pass if offered up for a vote in today's political climate.

Social Security, Unemployment Compensation and **Minimum Wages** are legislation that were passed in the depression to alleviate poverty and suffering among the elderly and the unemployed. These would be called liberal in today's political climate. Yet millions of Americans would not be able to survive without them. Another example of liberal legislation is **Medicare** and **Medicaid**, without which millions of Americans would be unable to see a doctor when they get sick.

(**Opinion**) *I believe that Americans are more liberal than they say they are. The arguments for this claim are that true conservatives would not want to keep liberal programs like social security, Medicare, Medicaid, unemployment compensation etc. Yet most Americans, when asked if they would like to see these liberal programs eliminated say they would not! This confusion between what people say and what they want stems from **ignorance** or a lack of **awareness.***

This observation reinforces the thesis that economic hard times make people more liberal and less conservative, simply because the more people become unemployed and poor, the greater they feel the need for government assistance for them to survive. This can be verified by actual research. Though informal, my research with students of Faulkner University has shown this to be true. Each semester I would ask my students in some of my macroeconomics classes if they considered themselves conservative or liberal. Almost all would say they were conservative. However, these same students, when asked if they would like to see the Congress eliminate programs like Social security, student loans, Medicare and Medicaid and unemployment compensation, would all say "**NO!**"

Why this divergence between what they say and what they actually want? This stems from a cultural habit of following in the political footsteps of their parents. The young are not aware that they are frequently voting against their own interests.

Phillip Gregorowicz, my now deceased friend and a former professor of economics at Auburn University Montgomery once told me, "**The civil rights movement saved the South.**" I asked him what he meant and he explained in the form of a question. He asked me, "**Do you think that Mercedes, Hyundai, Toyota and Honda would have ever built their multi billion dollar plants in the Jim Crow South?**" I was stunned and replied, "**I don't think they would have, any more than they would have wanted to make such massive investments in Apartheid South Africa!**"

To understand this requires a little history. In 1964, when a **Democratic President and Congress** passed the **voting rights** and **civil rights acts,** Lyndon Johnson lamented that "**We will lose the South for a generation.**" The South, just as Johnson had predicted, from that day on voted **Republican** to punish **Democrats** for doing the one thing that made the South a more palatable place for international investments. America passed laws that humanized the country and the **Democratic Party** was punished for it, even though the South benefitted with unprecedented economic development. Most people in the South have never made this connection between humane laws and huge international investments in the South. They continue to punish the **Democrats** for giving them a brighter future and a place in the twenty first century. I consider this an example of **ignorance or misinformation**!

As the current economic recession continues, and the auto industry in the north appears on the verge of collapse, the South stands to benefit even more from increased international investments. These were made possible by the civil rights laws that turned the South from a racial tinderbox into a more peaceful environment for attracting investments. The South, however is still punishing the **Democratic Party** for bringing them kicking and screaming into the twenty-first century.

CHAPTER SEVEN-
Productivity at the personal and national level

Productivity is the value of output per hour of labor. Over the past hundred years, American productivity has increased at an amazing rate, contributing to America becoming the richest country in the world, with one of the highest standards of living.

Technology is all of man's knowledge of how to produce. When new technology is invented, the nation's workers become more productive and individual incomes rise, business firm incomes rise, and national income rises. Most of the gains in productivity come from new and improved technology, but many gains can be attributed to better education and training

Sometime in the early twentieth century, America committed itself to the goal of better education for the entire population and funded public schools, both primary and secondary. They also made college education within the reach of most citizens through grants and college loan programs.

These efforts, funded by the taxpayers, have made American productivity one of the highest in the world, and American higher education one of the best in the world.

Because of access to higher education, immigrants from all over the world desire to come to America. I know this from personal experience because I am one. I came to America in 1970, attended college and attained a Master's Degree in Economics. But this investment in my education has resulted in benefits not only to me! These benefits can be seen in an ever-widening circle of students I have taught. I have contributed to the education of thousands of American and international students whom I have taught over the past twenty-six years. Many of the students have spread out around the country and the world, spreading the good news about the effectiveness of the Capitalist Model of economic development.

The point I truly want to impart is that the money spent on education is actually an investment in human capital; one that pays the highest return ever received by most people. The returns are enormous, and keep on coming even after death, because of its effects on the offspring of the educated.

But because of the political process involved in the allocation of revenue to government spending, many people fail to recognize the value of education and are unwilling to vote to fund it, mostly because of ignorance or misinformation! Are most Americans aware that the **GI Bill** made America the most educated people in the world? No place else in the world has as high a proportion of their population with college degrees as America. But the GI Bill, if it came up for funding today would probably be called socialism and would be voted down.

Quite a few of America's greatest achievements of the last century would not be voted for today, because they would be considered too socialistic. During the twentieth century, **America's greatest century**, the Congress passed legislation that benefitted most of the people, rich and poor. I wonder if people in this country would be happy if there was no **right to unionize**, no **unemployment relief**, no **worker's compensation**, no **social security**, no **Medicare** or **Medicaid**, no **Aid to Families with Dependent Children**! I doubt it! Yet most of these programs would be called socialism in today's political climate, and would have no chance of passing.

The world outside of these borders recognizes America's greatness not because of its powerful **Army, Navy and Air Force**. No! It is because of its humanity, its system of education, its courts, and its political system. But these extraordinary gifts are things that most Americans take for granted. Many people seem to have little understanding of these gifts, and show little appreciation for them.

The teaching of **Civics** in schools has been abandoned. Does America really want an uninformed electorate? Who would think that it's good political strategy to keep people ignorant and uninformed? It has to be ignorance that makes Americans say they are conservative, yet want to hold on to every liberal program just mentioned. Why would they be against programs that benefit most of the people? Ignorance will make people vote to cut the very programs that made this country the envy of the world. Those so-called liberal programs gave America one of the largest and wealthiest middle class groups in the world, but many Americans are unaware of this.

These statements are not simply **opinion. An impartial** investigation will reveal that these are historical facts that can be verified. American worker productivity can be verified by research. When political parties fail to fund progressive policies for short term political gain based on a hoodwinked electorate, this can only be harmful to America in its attempts to set a good example for the world.

Again I want to mention my friend the late Dr. Phil Gregorowicz, whose knowledge of economics has had a great influence on my thinking over the twenty-five years that I have known him. I once asked him why the American Corporate world approved of the huge payouts of salary and other remuneration to their CEO's while the working people, the average workers who do the actual work of the corporation find their pay flat or receding. His answer seemed quite full of wisdom. I thought of it for a long time and concluded that he was right. He said, **"These CEO's do this because they can. It has nothing to do with markets,"** (the usual justification given for such excesses.)

During the latter part of 2009 after the taxpayers had bailed out the financial industry, Congress tried to put in place legislation to prevent a repeat of the financial meltdown of 2008. The same companies that had been rescued by the taxpayers spent hundreds of millions of dollars in *bribes* to stop the legislation. That is not "markets at work"; that is a rank display of power that the corporations have over the American government. *We the people* have been sold out to the highest bidder, the **Financial Industry**.

In Japan, the excessive corporate pay is unheard of. Why? It is because Japan has an ancient and highly developed pre-capitalist society where social mores are more powerful than the desire for personal gratification. Their society considers such excessive greed as vulgar and un-Japanese. Such behavior would be looked down upon and practitioners of it would be ostracized by their peers, and disrespected by the entire Japanese society. America, on the other hand, has a young society with non-existent or weak pre-industrial social mores and attitudes. Americans revel in an **"every man for himself"** mentality.

Things that would embarrass Japanese would often find praise in this **Wild West** society; things such as people's demands that they be allowed to own and use assault weapons. I am a naturalized citizen of the country and am proud to call myself an **American**, but several recent developments are very disquieting. The increasing gap between the rich and the poor is quite startling, yet it goes largely unnoticed by the society. Just before the start of the Great Depression, the gap between the richest and the poorest Americans was the largest it had ever been. Legislation passed during and after the Great Depression closed much of that disparity. In 2008, it had again reached the same point as it had in 1929. Many recent political and economic movements such as tax policies have encouraged this increasing disparity, which the electorate seems to be unaware of.

Warren Buffett, the outspoken American billionaire was on television in 2008 lamenting that the tax system that favored the wealthy was wrong. He stated that he had paid 17% of his forty million dollar salary in taxes, while his secretary had paid 33% in taxes on her sixty thousand dollar income. He said that this was wrong, but most Americans didn't seem to pay attention to what he said.

Americans were justifiably angry when the leaders of the corporations that led the country to the brink of disaster in 2008 continued to receive massive bonuses, even higher than they had received in the previous year. Even CEO's and top managers of banks that received bailouts of billions of taxpayer dollars continued to receive huge bonuses. Auto workers and workers in other industries had to accept huge cuts in pay and benefits in order to receive bailout money. Why are bankers and investment CEO's treated with kid gloves? They didn't deserve the bonuses they had gotten in previous years, when their **short-term** horizons led them to begin taking excessive risks to justify overpaying themselves. After the economy collapsed and the truth came out, they should have been made to repay their ill gotten bonuses. Instead they were further rewarded for almost destroying the economy.

When informed by a bank official that the banks have to pay bonuses to keep their "Good" people, **Jon Stewart** of the popular **Daily Show** justifiably responded, **"But you don't have any good people!"** One can only assume that in America it is good corporate practice to reward CEO's for almost destroying the country's economy and blowing trillions of dollars of investor wealth. It is baffling, to say the least!

If the same rules were applied to teachers' performance, we would be paid the highest for putting out into society the most ignorant and untrained group of graduates in the history of the world. But the American public meekly sat back and let the Wall Street Barons get away with this **"legalized fraud."**

Instead, the people vent their anger at congressmen who are trying to pass legislation to help people who don't have health insurance. **"Divide and conquer"** is a very effective means for fooling an entire society!

CHAPTER EIGHT -
Some Common Fallacies Explained

If you watch television news you might hear conservative pundits say untrue things so often without being challenged that after a while you may accept that these statements must be true. One of the common fallacies that are repeated over and over without rebuff is the following.

> *"Cutting tax rates causes government tax revenue to rise."*

This is illogical and **counter intuitive**. Here is why! If cutting tax rates will cause government revenues to rise, why don't we try cutting the rate down to zero! This should cause government revenues to be infinite, if the argument holds true. The converse to this argument is: "If tax rates were to increase to 100%, government tax revenue would be zero because no one would have the incentive to produce anything." This is probably true, but no government has ever tried this, to my knowledge.

But there is another **empirical** reason why this is not true. For eight years the Bush government (2001- 2008) has cut tax rates, and all that has happened is that the national debt has gone from $5.5 trillion to nearly $11 trillion and the annual budget situation has gone from $200 billion **surplus** in 2000 to over $700 billion **deficit in 2008**.

I believe that these pundits misunderstand the Laffer curve, which demonstrates that "**when marginal tax rates are extremely high, cutting tax rates will result in increased revenue.**" But this is true only when marginal tax rates are very high, such as 70% as they were during the Reagan years. With the highest tax rate today being 35%, this argument makes no sense. These pundits on television continue spewing this non-logic anyway, and Americans continue to be influenced by a downright wrong argument.

Another fallacy that so called conservatives use is that "**the government does not create jobs**." Who then are all those millions of people who work for the government in the military and the government bureaucracy? Don't they have jobs? Or are they playing games and getting paid for it? This is ignorance being repeated by people who call themselves conservative but really don't have much common sense. Many Americans just accept as true anything that comes out of the mouth of their favorite pundits.

I believe that what these people who say that

government does not create jobs are actually trying to say is this: **"If the private sector did not create the economic activity that generated wealth and incomes, then the government would not have the tax revenue to pay the soldiers, bureaucrats, firemen, policemen, social security workers, Medicaid workers etc who work for the government."**

However, when they say that the government does not create jobs they are showing that they do not know anything about economics. A little bit of knowledge can be a dangerous thing!

Here is another fallacy that so-called conservatives believe and want to pass along to an unaware population.

"Government actions to help the people will hurt business."

When the American economy was rapidly slipping into the most severe recession since the Great Depression, many conservatives kept repeating that the government ought to stay out of the picture. They claim that it is bad for business. Which do you think is more important to America, its *people or its businesses?*

Before there was business, before there was capitalism, there were the *people*, and the people lived in a country called America. The Western countries, including America then created the system of economics called capitalism and free enterprise. Its purpose was to make life better for the *people* in the country. It was created to serve the needs of the *people*. The notion that *people* are there to serve business is nihilistic and illogical. Yet many Americans have accepted this twisted logic as if it were gospel.

Please take note of something about those persons who are seen on television complaining that the one sixth of the population with no health insurance should be left to fend for itself. Those people **all** tend to have great health insurance policies provided by their employers, but even if they didn't, they make enough money to buy the best healthcare that is available! These are smug, self-satisfied rich people who know nothing of the problems of ordinary people. They don't care about those less fortunate than themselves. One of the purposes of this book is to give people the tools to challenge those overpaid pundits who make such indefensible arguments.

Knowledge is the best antidote to counter the illogical statements made by people who think that their political agenda is more important than the welfare of ordinary Americans. Some people will say anything, no matter how false or nonsensical, to promote their own agenda, and neither truth nor logic has any place in their commentary.

Rush Limbaugh is a rich, powerful radio commentator who calls himself a conservative spokesman. I am willing to bet that he does not have one friend who is poor. He is insensitive to anyone who doesn't think like him. Yet there are millions of people, rich and poor, black and white who listen to his inflammatory statements and accept them like words from God.

This man is rich enough to buy an island for himself and his family if the American economy goes bust. His salary is reported to be about $400 million over the next six years. If he were to work 40 hours per week for eight hours per day (I know he doesn't work such long hours) he would be making $32,000 per hour! How many of his listeners make even twenty dollars per hour? Not too many, I'd surmise!

Any politician who says something in the media contrary to Limbaugh's beliefs is often found begging for his forgiveness the next day, because he wields great power and so-called conservative politicians fear him. Though I believe that everyone, including Limbaugh has the right to his opinion, I believe that American people ought to ask themselves if commentators like him have the common people's interests at heart.

I find myself mostly sympathetic to the plight of the poor because I was born in poverty in a poor county. Most of my ideas have been influenced by my birth and upbringing. Just as I can't help my feelings of concern for the poor, the affluent can't help their identification with the rich, because their friends are rich and their life experience has been shaped by their affluence.

I have heard this statement often, though I don't know where it came from; **"You can't understand my life until you've walked a mile in my shoes."** People can't help who they are sympathetic to any more than they can shrug off their culture. When I was a child in the forties and fifties, my fourteen siblings and I thought it was quite a treat to get a drink of milk. When I saw my daughter in the nineteen eighties throwing away the milk left over after she had eaten the cereal in her bowl, I was flabbergasted.

She also thought it was ok to fill a washing machine up with water to wash a pair of her shoelaces. I didn't blame her! She was raised in relative affluence because her mother and I always had good jobs when she was a child. She was behaving like all the kids of her generation who were raised in relative affluence. However, we did teach her to also try to see the world through the eyes of her poorer relatives in Guyana who had few of the benefits that she had.

What makes me uneasy is when people believe without reservation, unfeeling statements coming from people who have never been poor, and who show little sympathy for people not of their level of affluence. My friend Phil Gregorowicz used to say that George Bush was being faithful to his class when he cut taxes for the richest Americans. He didn't blame Bush for this, even though Bush had taken a vow to be the president of all Americans.

Bush knew that many poor and middle class Americans would vote for him even though he was promoting legislation that benefitted them little, but was mostly for the rich. He knew that an uninformed electorate could be led anywhere he chose to lead them. Maybe the American middle class, whose incomes have remained flat throughout the Bush presidency, believed that they would all become fabulously rich one day and would benefit from his largesse.

CHAPTER NINE -
Healthcare, does it need fixing?

In the summer of 2009 the US Congress made a decision to do something about the nation's healthcare system. Why? Was something wrong with healthcare in America? Many readers may be thinking, "**But don't we have the best healthcare system in the world?**" Well, they are right, we do, but for people who are rich, or are covered by very good health insurance plans. And even for those with adequate health insurance plans, **medical bankruptcy** has been occurring recently at a rate of hundreds of thousands per year. For those people who are neither rich nor possess good health insurance, the situation is a problem. But why is that so? Because America, (**unlike Canada, England and most of Europe**), has a privately run, **for profit** health insurance system. People who aren't insured through their jobs have to buy health insurance on the **open market**. It is quite expensive and out of the reach of most Americans. So the problem facing Congress in 2009 was to find a way of insuring the 16% of Americans who have no insurance.

Are you thinking, "But surely we don't let the poor die if they get sick and don't have insurance, do we?" Well, no! The poor and uninsured usually wait until their illness gets to the **emergency** stage. Then they go to the **emergency room** at the hospital, where they can't be refused treatment. It is illegal for a hospital to refuse to treat a person in an emergency, so an uninsured person's first contact with a doctor is often in the **ER**. But who pays for that? Well, the hospital charges the 84% who have health insurance for the unpaid bills of the uninsured 16%. **So it is true that everyone in America, including the poor and the uninsured do eventually get healthcare.** They get it in the ER, which just happens to be **the most expensive form of treatment**. In addition, waiting until a condition reaches a critical point before seeing a doctor often ends in premature death. It was recently reported in a Harvard University study that **44,000 Americans die prematurely each year because of not having health insurance.**

But is America satisfied with this arrangement? Is there an urgent need to fix the system? **"If it ain't broke, don't fix it!"** as the saying goes. The problem is that even if we are happy with things **today,** we won't be happy in a few years. At an eight percent annual increase in the cost of medical care, (the current rate of increase) healthcare expenditures will double from 16% of GDP today to 32% of GDP by 2019. How do I know that this will happen by 2019? It is easily calculated with the Rule of 72.

(The rule of 72 is a mathematical identity that shows that something growing at the rate of x% /period will double in 72/x periods. For example, if healthcare cost rises at 8% per year, the cost will double every 72/8 = 9 years. To test this, take a calculator, put in $100, and then multiply it by1.08. The answer is $108. Multiply each successive answer by 1.08 eight more times. The result is $199.90, about double what you started with)

If in 2019, 32% of GDP will be represented by healthcare, how can we afford to pay for it? By most estimates we won't. People will still have to provide housing, food, transportation, clothing etc for their existence. Today the average household is living to the hilt of its income. At this rate Americans in 2019 will have to cut back severely on housing, food, transportation and everything else just to pay for healthcare.

This situation is **unsustainable** and has to be fixed soon. The Congress has been trying to create healthcare **options,** but many of the people who stand to benefit from this action are against it. This is so not because they don't want help or need help, but because they have been persuaded to oppose it by the use of the same buzz words that were used to rile up Americans against Russia during the cold war. During this period, 1945 through 1989, the word **socialism** was used to mean something evil and sinister that was associated with Russia,

China, Cuba and other socialist countries**. In today's politics the word refers to any program provided by the government, and this also has taken on a negative connotation.

Even Americans who are enjoying the benefits of healthcare provided by the government are speaking out against **"Government Socialism."** Many of the elderly who are receiving Social Security and Medicare are being encouraged to speak out against the same program that is sustaining them. It is like the cartoon character that is sawing a tree limb on which he is standing!

The present amount of ignorance and deliberate misinformation in healthcare is astounding. Can this avalanche of misinformation be turned back? Only time will tell! I don't think that many of the elderly know that they are condemning the same program that is making their old age bearable. When I look at the situation, the choices available to America are:

1)Let things remain as they are and let healthcare payments consume more than 50% of our household spending in the next 20 years. I don't think many people will like that.

2)Let a government-run insurance company provide an alternative choice to monopolized private health insurance (called the public option) and let it compete with the insurance companies to make them more competitive and make prices decrease. *(Doesn't competition always cause a lowering of prices?)**

3) *Let the government provide all healthcare to all Americans such as is done in England and Canada (called a single payer system)*

Which of these choices will the people most likely want? If Americans received all the facts and **believed** them, they will most likely go for **choice 2**. Why do I think so? Because **choice 1**) is totally unsustainable and the country will go broke paying for healthcare. The **third choice** is not likely to be chosen because the minds of Americans have been so thoroughly poisoned against what is called **socialized medicine** that most Americans will balk at it. The American media frequently reports that the Canadian and the English healthcare systems have resulted in people having no choices and having to wait months to see a doctor. I don't believe any of it because I have asked many Canadians and British subjects about it. They all say that they like and want to hold on to their system. They think that America's system was created for the rich and that America cares little what happens to the poor.

America won't accept choice 3 because they are suspicious of all government programs they see as representing socialism. But are most Americans aware that **defense, police, fire protection, public** schools, social security, Medicare, public health programs etc are all provided by some level of government? Shouldn't they reject all these programs for being socialized?

Maybe the **Cold War** anti-communist propaganda forces were so successful in convincing Americans to reject all things associated with the **Soviet (Communist)** system that we have thrown away the good with the bad. I fear that our mistrust of socialism has made us reject many of the programs that made America great in the past, all in the interest in fighting a battle that we won two decades ago.

Recently my wife told me of a friend who complained to her that she didn't like the idea of socialism in America's healthcare system. The friend then admitted that her medical insurance is provided and subsidized by the State of Alabama. *My wife then quietly explained to her that the health insurance she has already is socialism! (according to the conservative's definition of socialism) She had no answer to that!*

*

In the nineteen seventies, with only one telephone company operating in America, (**AT&T**), long distance phone calls within America's borders cost $.35 to $.45 per minute. Today, with thousands of competitors in the telephone and communications industry, the cost of a long distance call is a fraction of a cent per minute. **Competition does work!!**

**

In 1989 the Berlin Wall crumbled and East German residents swarmed into West Germany. This symbolized the end of the Cold War and of the Soviet Union. The Soviet Union broke up into Russia and a bunch of smaller republics, all of which started attempting to create economic systems modeled on the capitalist system. *Capitalism had won and Socialism had failed!*

CHAPTER TEN -
Does it matter if we receive news or opinion from the media?

For generations Americans watched the news provided by the three major television networks, CBS, NBC and ABC. These organizations were staffed with professional journalists who took pride in providing objective news to the people. Opinions were rarely expressed except in specific parts of a news program where senior editorial writers were given the opportunity to express their opinions. There was no confusing news with editorial content.

In recent years, however, it has become more prevalent for news anchors, reporters and other talking heads to clutter the airwaves with their opinions throughout the day, with no effort to separate news from editorial. As a result, some (so-called) news organizations report opinions and editorial as if they were straight news. This is a significant departure from the days when news was presented strictly as news.

How did this happen and is it important to again separate the news from opinion? Many respected journalists have lamented the recent breakdown of news into opinion in some of the largest media organizations in America. Many such organizations pay huge salaries to people who spend all their time saying anything they want with little regard for accuracy or journalistic standards.

These persons are often untrained as journalists but become popular with their particular audiences and make money for the media organizations they work for. But are they helping the political discourse in America? I don't think so. I see them as creating confusion and making people less informed. Their purpose seems to be to enrage people by appealing to the part of their psyche that is most vulnerable to manipulation, no matter how illogical the arguments they use.

Media organizations also appeal to celebrities (those who share their anger at the government) to come on their programs to stir up anti- government sentiment, sometimes with laughable results. Craig T Nelson, star of the nineties sitcom "Coach" recently stated that he doesn't need the government interfering in his affairs. He said, **"I've been on food stamps and welfare. Did anybody help me out? No!"** I wonder if he has since learned that the welfare and food stamps that sustained him during his poverty days came from the same government that he now disdains!

Another uninformed person speaking at a town hall meeting to discuss healthcare reform stated that she wanted the government to **"Keep your government hands off my Medicare**." Sometimes it makes me cringe to hear such absurdities, but in a democracy each person is entitled to his view, no matter how illogical or uninformed it is.

I think that the Founding Fathers understood that for a democracy to function efficiently, the populace must be well informed about conditions and events surrounding them. Well, I think that the Founding Fathers would be very disappointed if they were alive to see the rampant ignorance and misinformation that suffuses the current discourse. It has been recently revealed that the conservatives in the nineteen sixties objected to Medicare when it was proposed. Today, however, America is lucky that such programs exist. If it were not for Social Security and Medicare, the suffering among the poor and elderly today would be worse than during the Great Depression.

There are some Americans who believe that letting each individual make all of the decisions about his future will result in the best outcomes for the entire society. **Adam Smith**, the founder of modern economics believed that an "invisible hand" would guide people to make the best decisions for society under such an arrangement. What Smith failed to realize was that two centuries later the society would prove by its own actions that it would not work in some situations.

Suppose every American had been given the freedom to choose whether or not to invest part of their income into social security at its inception. Suppose half had accepted the offer in the 1930's and the other half had chosen not to join. Would one expect those Americans who had chosen not to pay into social security to be better off when they reached age sixty-five? Based on the savings rate of Americans, (zero percent as of a year ago), most would be facing a bleak old age! Investment manuals usually state, correctly, that money invested in the stock market over the period between 1925 and 2005 would give the investor a bright future. However, a person who spends all of his income would be excluded from that bright future. *You have to save money in order to invest money!*

Because of employer-based retirement programs and tax incentives to save for retirement, some Americans have retirement incomes to look forward to. The number of people who are financially ill prepared for old age is still quite staggering, however. Add to that the fact that the wipeout in the stock market in 2008 has made millions of people have to put off retirement indefinitely.

During the period 2004 thru 2005, attempts were made to permit social security payments to be invested into the stock market. If that attempt had succeeded, the recent stock market crash would have wiped out additional trillions of Americans' wealth along with the trillions already gone.

There was a strategy used during slavery to keep slaves from uniting to rebel against their masters. The strategy was called "**Divide and Conquer**." What that means is to keep slaves so busy fighting among themselves that they had no energy or impetus to come together to fight a common enemy, the slaveholder. During colonial times, the British used it to keep colonists fighting over petty issues while they (the British) continued to exploit the colony's natural resources.

Today, that same strategy is being used to keep Americans from uniting to fight against those forces responsible for concentrating the wealth into fewer and fewer hands. *The strategy is to divide Americans into Republicans and Democrats who hate one another so much that they can be easily manipulated.* In the meantime, a new form of **robber baron**, one that appears above suspicion, is robbing Americans blind!

During the eighties and nineties when the **wealth concentration** first became noticeable, people showed no interest in finding out about it. To make clearer what is meant by **wealth concentration**, the average CEO of a major company in the nineteen sixties made about 40 times the average worker. In 2009 the average CEO makes about 350 to 400 times the average worker. Yet most Americans ignore this while venting their venom on the particular political party that they blame for their lives not being what they want them to be.

They are so busy hating either Republicans or Democrats that they are unaware that *their country is being stolen from them right under their noses*!! This situation is a prime example of an uninformed and hoodwinked electorate being manipulated by various groups of clever people. At the health care town hall meetings previously mentioned, people stood and shouted their anger at the speakers, making it impossible for any information to be passed along. Part of the reason for the anger is the political pundits in the media filling them with misinformation that they never verify, but accept whole-heartedly.

There was such an example on the **Daily Show** of August 20, 2009. A pundit called Betsy McCaughey repeatedly stated that the health care bill proposed by Congress included instructions to kill the elderly to save money. Despite the fact that Stewart continued to repeat the passage from the legislation, she insisted that the statement meant, "To kill the elderly." (The passage read in part "Such measures shall measure both the creation and adherence to orders for **life sustaining** treatment.")

Betsy McCaughey interestingly interpreted that statement to mean that the legislation was meant to kill old people. She still continues to go on television repeating this lie, and has convinced millions of elderly Americans to fear the legislation. Is there anything that can be done to discourage people with an agenda from lying to Americans? Only time will tell!!

CHAPTER ELEVEN -
Summing up

This book makes an attempt to explain economics and its ramifications for average Americans. Its purpose is to provide facts and arguments to encourage Americans to think for themselves, to question sweeping statements with skepticism until they have examined the logic and the facts. Dr John Allen Paulos, author of **"Innumeracy, the mathematical equivalent of illiteracy,"** stated that one of the unexpected benefits of understanding mathematics is a tendency to be skeptical of myths and legends. **When things don't add up, don't believe them!**

Several years ago a story was flying around the internet that the clothing designer Tommy Hilfiger had stated on the Oprah Winfrey Show that **"if he had know that black people would have been so attracted to his fashions, he would not have made them so well."** Many black Americans believed this and pledged to never buy Hilfiger clothes. When I asked my friend Phil what he thought about it, he said, "I don't believe that a sane and successful entrepreneur would say things to cut his own throat." I agreed with Phil that this was nonsense and dismissed the whole rumor.

I understand that Oprah was finally persuaded to issue a statement that Hilfiger had never been a guest on her show. It was all a prank or whatever you call the spreading of destructive rumors. But millions of black Americans actually believed it.

If Americans of all races, ages and cultures would stop being so **gullible** and start dismissing statements that make no sense, the public discourse would be much more informative and would help people to make decisions in their own self interest. During the summer of 2009 there were rumors that healthcare legislation was being considered to kill the elderly. It made so sense and an examination of the legislation could have quickly cleared it up. Millions of Americans, however, believed the lie and became afraid that the government wanted to kill their grandparents. Part of the reason that this lie had such an effect was that many of the politicians, who had earlier supported legislation for "end of life" consultations, started repeating the lie for their own ends. Such politicians should be made to pay a price for lying to the people.

In September 2009, when President Obama wanted to talk to students about staying in school and studying hard to improve their future and their country's future, people vociferously revolted, calling it indoctrination of their children. This seems to me to be one of the most egregious examples of some members of the society being manipulated for a political agenda not of their choosing, and not in their interest. I can't recall any greater example of fear tactics being used to blatantly rile up a misguided electorate. Parents would do well to take as much time monitoring what their children watch on **MTV** and on the **World Wide Webb**!

If I could persuade just one person in this country to start demanding the facts, verifying sources of information and applying common sense to every discussion, this book would not have been written in vain. If this book could be placed in the hands of students from elementary to college, the next generation of Americans might be persuaded to **read more, ask more questions and be more skeptical of statements that make no sense, regardless of who made them!**

THE END

GLOSSARY OF TERMS

Abundant – Being available in large quantities

Accumulating – Gathering up and collecting

Advertising – Activities intended to inform people about goods and to get people to buy them

Aid to Families with Dependent Children - Federal Government program that gives food stamps and other financial help to poor families with young children

Baby Boomers – The group of people who were born beginning around the end of the Second World War until the early sixties

Bankrupt – A situation when a bank or business fails and cannot meet its obligations. It usually goes out of business

Barter – The act of exchanging goods directly for other goods without benefit of a medium like money

Benefits – Better working conditions that workers

desire, such as sick leave, paid vacation time and safe surroundings

Budget deficit – The annual amount by which government spending exceeds tax revenues received by the government

Budget Surplus – When the federal government collects more tax revenue than the amount of money they spend in a year

Business cycle – The historical rises and falls in production that occurs over a period of years in an economy

Business firms – Any entity that is conducting business in an economy. It could be an individual, a partnership or a corporation

Capital – all goods that are used to produce something, including tools, factories, technology and money

Capitalism – An economic system in which goods are mostly produced by privately owned companies

Civics – The study of citizens and government with particular attention to the role of citizens in the governing of a country

Cold War – The period of time (1945 through 1989) when America and the West were in a state of constant tension against China, Russia and the Soviet Bloc of countries in Eastern Europe

Commercials – Activities shown on television or magazines intended to get people to buy things

Commodity – Any item useful for meeting our everyday needs such as corn, wheat, meat, fish etc

Common Sense – Appealing to the everyday thinking of ordinary people

Conservative – A person who thinks that the government ought to play a limited role in people's lives, leaving them to fend for themselves

Consumers – People who want goods and are willing to pay for them

Convenience – Anything that makes doing an action easier and less troublesome

Convulsions – The disruptions in the economy that make living difficult

Currency – Another name for money

Cyclical unemployment – Unemployment caused by the economy going into a recession

Decisions – Making up one's mind about what to do in any particular situation

Defense – The act of protecting the country from any group or country that wants to do it harm

Demand and Supply – The system in economics dealing with what people want (demand) and what producers make for them (supply).

Democrat – One of the two dominant political parties in America, usually considered the more liberal party

Demystify – the act of removing the mystery around an idea

Desirable – When the economy is working the way policy makers want it to work, with low unemployment and low inflation

Dishonor – The idea of doing things that society considers bad or immoral

Disposable income – The income that remains after people have paid their income taxes

Divide and Conquer – a philosophy of control based on keeping subjects fighting among themselves in order to minimize the chance that they would form an effective alliance

Double Coincidence of wants - For barter to take place, each person must want what the other person has to trade

ER – Emergency Room- that part of a hospital specially equipped and staffed to deal with medical emergencies

Economy – The system by which countries provide for the needs of their citizens

Efficient – Getting much output in return for little input

Elasticity of Demand – A measure of how consumers react when the price of a good changes

Emergency – A situation where a person's illness is very serious and life threatening

Entrepreneurship – The skill or ability to manage a business, especially when one owns the business

Environment – The circumstances or conditions surrounding a person or place

FDIC – The Federal Deposit Insurance Corporation – an agency of the Federal Reserve System responsible for insuring the deposits of savers in certain banks

Federal Budget Deficit – The amount of yearly federal government spending that exceeds yearly tax revenues

Federal Government – The part of the government that is responsible for the overall welfare of the country

Federal Reserve System - A system of banks created in 1913 by the Congress to regulate America's banks, manage monetary policy and keep the financial system operating properly

Fiscal policy – The use of taxes and federal government spending to regulate the nation's economy

Foreclosure – The legal act of taking the property of someone who fails to make the required payments on their mortgage loan

Foreign sector – That part of the economy made up of purchases by Americans of goods made overseas (imports) and goods made in America and purchased by foreign countries (exports)

For profit – A business or organization the primary purpose of which is to make profit for its shareholders or owners

Frictional unemployment – Unemployment of people who are temporarily between jobs

Generation – A period of time it takes a group of people born around the same time to have and raise a family, called the next generation

GI Bill – A federal government program that pays for college tuition and makes housing loans for veterans of the military

Goldsmith – A person who fashions gold into ornaments or other items (in the Middle Ages they became the forerunners of today's banks)

Government spending – The spending on goods and services done by the federal government

Great Depression – The period of time (1929 thru 1941) in which the world economy shrank by the greatest proportion ever known

Gross Domestic Product – The total value of all final goods produced in a year

Groupthink – (from the novel **"1984"**, by George Orwell.) The process of giving up individual thinking and accepting the thoughts and ideas promoted by a political group

Gullible – easily deceived or duped

Honor – An idea of doing what one considers the right thing

Household – A group of people who live together as a family

Ignorance – The state or condition of being unaware or not knowing

Immigrants – People who come into a country from other countries to live

Impartial – Not subject to political bias in rendering an opinion

Income – the amount of money that people earn over a period of time

Income Taxes – Taxes that people pay based on the amount of money they earn each year

Inflation – When the average prices of most things bought by households rise

Instructor – teacher, usually at the college level

Interest – The payment received by the owners of capital (money) when they lend or lease it to others

Interest rates – The rates at which people borrow money from banks and other financial institutions

Intimidating – Scary or tending to make one feel overwhelmed

Introductory – Beginner's course, taught at a level for beginners

Investment – The spending done by business firms in the production of goods and services

Keynes – **(John Maynard)** a respected British economist who advised the American government during the Great Depression

Labor – Paid human effort; people who are paid a wage to do a task

Land – The surface of the earth and all that stands on it

Law of diminishing marginal utility – The idea that when a person consumes more units of a good, each successive unit gives less satisfaction than the previous unit

Leasing – The process of letting another use an asset temporarily for a price

Left – Liberals

Legalized Fraud – Between 1999 and 2008, banking and investment managers gambled with depositors' money, irresponsibly and knowingly taking big risks and making huge but unsustainable profits, then paid themselves large salaries. After the crash, they kept their money while the American people lost most of their wealth. *It should have been illegal, but it was not!*

Liberal – A person who thinks that government ought to intervene to provide for certain basic needs of citizens

Local Government – The part of the government that is responsible for the welfare of the cities and counties

Logical – Appealing to a sense of logic or reasoning

Loss – The money lost when a business finds its expenses greater that its sales revenue

MTV – Music Television: Many of the videos are adult fare and unsuitable for young viewers

Markets – The system of laws, rules and customs that govern the buying and selling of goods and services in a capitalist economy, with no government intervention

Manageable debt – Amount of debt that a person or government can afford to pay without great stress to their budget

Marginal Tax Rates – The rate of taxes paid on the last dollar of income earned, as opposed to the average tax rate, which is the average of all rates, starting with the smallest rate charged on the first dollar of taxable income

Marketing - The process of informing people about goods and getting the goods into the hands of the people

Medicaid – A federal program that provides medical assistance to people who fall below a certain income level

Medical Bankruptcy – a situation where the cost of healthcare causes a person to declare bankruptcy

Medicare – A federal insurance program into which workers pay money and at retirement receive medical benefits

Medium of exchange – Money is used as a go-between when trading goods for goods

Methods of production – All the ways that people find to produce things

Minimum Wages – A federal law that mandates that a worker must be paid no less than a certain hourly wage

Monetary policy - The Federal Reserve's use of money supply and interest rates to regulate the economy

Monopolized Health Insurance – The health insurance industry in America is run by a set of large companies each of which represents an 80 to 95% share of the industry in each state. This means that most companies have no competition and can charge as much as they can get from buyers

Mystical – Something that is not of this world, difficult to understand

National Debt – The total amount of money owed by the federal government to all lenders, both domestic and foreign

Necessity – Something that people feel that they must have

Non-market – Using the government rather that depending on consumers and producers to solve a problem

Non-partisan–Not identifying with the philosophy of any of the dominant political parties

Open Market – Buying healthcare as an individual without the benefit of lower group pricing as is given to large companies and government agencies

Options - Choices

Outfit – To get all the troops ready for war and equipped with everything they need including food, weapons, housing, transportation etc

Panic – Fear that occurs when people lose faith in their banks and that makes them try to remove all their money

Partisanship – The process of thinking based on affiliation or identification with a dominant political party (Democrat or Republican)

Pearl Harbor – An American base in Hawaii that was attacked on December 7, 1941 by Japanese planes

Personal taxes – The taxes paid by citizens out of their incomes

Pessimism – A feeling among citizens that the economy is getting worse rather than better

Policy makers – The people like government officials who make decisions on behalf of the governed

Politics – The art or methods of conducting government

Poor – Having little wealth or income

Predictable – Being able to anticipate how people will behave

Price – An agreement on how much money consumers are willing to pay for something and how much producers are willing to sell it for

Priorities – The process of determining what is most important to people in society

Producers – People who make goods to sell to others for a profit

Productivity – Output per hour of work

Profit – The revenue received in excess of the costs of producing goods for sale

Property taxes – Taxes that people pay based on the value of land and buildings that they own

Recession – A situation when the economy goes into a slowdown in spending and unemployment rises

Republican – One of the two dominant political

parties in America, usually considered the more conservative party

Reserves – That part of the gold deposited with goldsmiths that is not lent out but held in case depositors need it

Revenue – The money received by the government from taxes paid by citizens

Right – conservatives

Right to Unionize – Laws that guarantee employee's rights to form unions

Robber Baron – In the 1800's, robber baron was an insulting term implying that a person used unfair business practices and showed little sensitivity to the common worker

Sales Taxes – Taxes that are paid on all things that people buy in stores

Satisfaction – The joy or pleasure people get from consuming a good

Saving – The act of not spending a part of one's income or earnings

Scarcity – Having a limited and small amount of something

Securities – Any of a number of debt instruments used by the government to borrow money

Second World War – The conflict between most industrialized nations of the world between 1938 and 1945

Self –interest – What is considered good for an individual who is making a choice

Short Term – a period of time too short to fully recognize the consequences of one's actions

Single Payer System – A program where the government pays for everyone's healthcare through tax revenues. Rich and poor get the same quality of care

Socialism – An economic system in which goods are mostly produced by the government

Socialized Medicine – medical care provided by the government of a country and paid for with tax dollars

Social Security – A federal program started during the Great Depression into which workers pay money and at retirement they receive payments

Soviet – During the cold war (1945 to 1991) Russia and about twenty other countries formed a political union which was called the **Union of Soviet Socialist Republics (USSR)**

State Government – The part of the government that is responsible for the welfare of the states

Stimulating – When the government spends money to get the economy moving at a faster rate after it goes into a recession

Stock Market Crash – In October 1929 the US stock market "crashed" as stocks lost a great deal of value as their prices fell precipitously, causing many rich people to become poor overnight. The crash had been preceded by excessive borrowing, excessive risk taking and huge but unsustainable profits. This is similar to what happened in 2008!

Store of Value – The value of money is not only for present use, but also for saving for future use. This is much more convenient than storing up meat or fish for use at a later date

Strike – When workers refuse to work unless their demands are met

Structural unemployment – Unemployment of people whose skills do not match the needs of the labor market

Taxes – The money that citizens are asked to pay in order to fund the various levels of government

Trade Union – An organization created to fight for the rights of workers to receive better pay and benefits

Trillion – One thousand billion, or a million million

Unemployment – That part of the labor force that is seeking and can't find work

Unit of Account – One of the three functions of money. It means that all goods are priced in money rather than in terms of other goods

Unsustainable - occurring at a rate that is impossible to continue

Wages – the payment one receives for selling one's labor

Wealth – The amount of valuable things that a person owns such as money, homes, cars, land etc.

Well-informed voters – voters who are knowledgeable about the economy and other issues of importance to them

West – the part of the world including North

America and Western Europe that is traditionally capitalistic

Workers Compensation – Federal insurance that makes payments to workers who are injured on the job

Workforce – All persons sixteen and older who are available and looking for work

World Wide Web – The worldwide internet, which provides online access to material much of which is very unsuitable for young viewers

Dr Philip Gregorowicz, to whom this book is dedicated, was born in Poland in 1945. His parents brought him to the United States when he was about five years old. He grew up in Chicago, Illinois where he attended Northern Illinois University and earned a PHD in Economics. In 1980 he started teaching at Auburn University at Montgomery, Alabama. I met him when I accepted a job there in 1983. He and I became friends who were as close as brothers, and shared many enjoyable days talking about economics, politics and a wide variety of topics. He read extensively and was a wonderful teacher. I learned a great deal from him, and many of his ideas are mentioned in this book.

When he died in August of 2008, he left behind his wife Jeanne and two daughters Krysha and Sonja, all of whom he loved dearly. I think of him often and thank him for his friendship and inspiration. I will miss him for the rest of my life.